# Francis Frith's
# AROUND SURREY

◆

PHOTOGRAPHIC MEMORIES

# Francis Frith's
# AROUND SURREY

◆

Helen Livingston

First published in the United Kingdom in 1999 by
Frith Book Company Ltd
ISBN 1-85937-081-0

Hardback edition reprinted in 2000
ISBN 1-85937-081-0

Paperback edition published in the United Kingdom in 2000 by
Frith Book Company Ltd
ISBN 1-85937-240-6

Paperback edition reprinted in 2000
ISBN 1-85937-240-6

Hardback edition reprinted in 2001
ISBN 1-85937-081-0

British Library Cataloguing in Publication Data

Francis Frith's Surrey
Helen Livingston

Frith Book Company Ltd
Frith's Barn, Teffont,
Salisbury, Wiltshire SP3 5QP
Tel: +44 (0) 1722 716 376
Email: info@frithbook.co.uk
www.frithbook.co.uk

Printed and bound in Great Britain

*Front Cover:* Caterham, A Motor 'Bus 1925  53334a

AS WITH ANY HISTORICAL DATABASE THE FRITH ARCHIVE IS CONSTANTLY BEING CORRECTED AND IMPROVED
AND THE PUBLISHERS WOULD WELCOME INFORMATION ON OMISSIONS OR INACCURACIES

# CONTENTS

# FRANCIS FRITH: *Victorian Pioneer*

FRANCIS FRITH, Victorian founder of the world-famous photographic archive, was a complex and multitudinous man. A devout Quaker and a highly successful Victorian businessman, he was both philosophic by nature and pioneering in outlook.

By 1855 Francis Frith had already established a wholesale grocery business in Liverpool, and sold it for the astonishing sum of £200,000, which is the equivalent today of over £15,000,000. Now a multi-millionaire, he was able to indulge his passion for travel. As a child he had pored over travel books written by early explorers, and his fancy and imagination had been stirred by family holidays to the sublime mountain regions of Wales and Scotland. 'What a land of spirit-stirring and enriching scenes and places!' he had written. He was to return to these scenes of grandeur in later years to 'recapture the thousands of vivid and tender memories', but with a different purpose. Now in his thirties, and captivated by the new science of photography, Frith set out on a series of pioneering journeys to the Nile regions that occupied him from 1856 until 1860.

## INTRIGUE AND ADVENTURE

He took with him on his travels a specially-designed wicker carriage that acted as both dark-room and sleeping chamber. These far-flung journeys were packed with intrigue and adventure. In his life story, written when he was sixty-three, Frith tells of being held captive by bandits, and of fighting 'an awful midnight battle to the very point of surrender with a deadly pack of hungry, wild dogs'. Sporting flowing Arab costume, Frith arrived at Akaba by camel seventy years before Lawrence, where he encountered 'desert princes and rival sheikhs, blazing with jewel-hilted swords'.

During these extraordinary adventures he was assiduously exploring the desert regions bordering the Nile and patiently recording the antiquities and peoples with his camera. He was the first photographer to venture beyond the sixth cataract. Africa was still the mysterious 'Dark Continent', and Stanley and Livingstone's historic meeting was a decade into the future. The conditions for picture taking confound belief. He laboured for hours in his wicker dark-room in the sweltering heat of the desert, while the volatile chemicals fizzed dangerously in their trays. Often he was forced to work in remote tombs and caves

where conditions were cooler. Back in London he exhibited his photographs and was 'rapturously cheered' by members of the Royal Society. His reputation as a photographer was made overnight. An eminent modern historian has likened their impact on the population of the time to that on our own generation of the first photographs taken on the surface of the moon.

## VENTURE OF A LIFE-TIME

Characteristically, Frith quickly spotted the opportunity to create a new business as a specialist publisher of photographs. He lived in an era of immense and sometimes violent change. For the poor in the early part of Victoria's reign work was a drudge and the hours long, and people had precious little free time to enjoy themselves.

Most had no transport other than a cart or gig at their disposal, and had not travelled far beyond the boundaries of their own town or village. However, by the 1870s, the railways had threaded their way across the country, and Bank Holidays and half-day Saturdays had been made obligatory by Act of Parliament. All of a sudden the ordinary working man and his family were able to enjoy days out and see a little more of the world.

With characteristic business acumen, Francis Frith foresaw that these new tourists would enjoy having souvenirs to commemorate their days out. In 1860 he married Mary Ann Rosling and set out with the intention of photographing every city, town and village in Britain. For the next thirty years he travelled the country by train and by pony and trap, producing fine photographs of seaside resorts and beauty spots that were keenly bought by millions of Victorians. These prints were painstakingly pasted into family albums and pored over during the dark nights of winter, rekindling precious memories of summer excursions.

## THE RISE OF FRITH & CO

Frith's studio was soon supplying retail shops all over the country. To meet the demand he gathered about him a small team of photographers, and published the work of independent artist-photographers of the calibre of Roger Fenton and Francis Bedford. In order to gain some understanding of the scale of Frith's business one only has to look at the catalogue issued by Frith & Co in 1886: it runs to some 670

pages, listing not only many thousands of views of the British Isles but also many photographs of most European countries, and China, Japan, the USA and Canada – note the sample page shown above from the hand-written *Frith & Co* ledgers detailing pictures taken. By 1890 Frith had created the greatest specialist photographic publishing company in the world, with over 2,000 outlets – more than the combined number that Boots and WH Smith have today! The picture on the right shows the *Frith & Co* display board at Ingleton in the Yorkshire Dales. Beautifully constructed with mahogany frame and gilt inserts, it could display up to a dozen local scenes.

## POSTCARD BONANZA

The ever-popular holiday postcard we know today took many years to develop. In 1870 the Post Office issued the first plain cards, with a pre-printed stamp on one face. In 1894 they allowed other publishers' cards to be sent through the mail with an attached adhesive halfpenny stamp. Demand grew rapidly, and in 1895 a new size of postcard was permitted called the

court card, but there was little room for illustration. In 1899, a year after Frith's death, a new card measuring 5.5 x 3.5 inches became the standard format, but it was not until 1902 that the divided back came into being, with address and message on one face and a full-size illustration on the other. *Frith & Co* were in the vanguard of postcard development, and Frith's sons Eustace and Cyril continued their father's monumental task, expanding the number of views offered to the public and recording more and more places in Britain, as the coasts and countryside were opened up to mass travel.

Francis Frith died in 1898 at his villa in Cannes, his great project still growing. The archive he created continued in business for another seventy years. By 1970 it contained over a third of a million pictures of 7,000 cities, towns and villages. The massive photographic record Frith has left to us stands as a living monument to a special and very remarkable man.

# Frith's Archive: *A Unique Legacy*

FRANCIS FRITH'S legacy to us today is of immense significance and value, for the magnificent archive of evocative photographs he created provides a unique record of change in 7,000 cities, towns and villages throughout Britain over a century and more. Frith and his fellow studio photographers revisited locations many times down the years to update their views, compiling for us an enthralling and colourful pageant of British life and character.

We tend to think of Frith's sepia views of Britain as nostalgic, for most of us use them to conjure up memories of places in our own lives with which we have family associations. It often makes us forget that to Francis Frith they were records of daily life as it was actually being lived in the cities, towns and villages of his day. The Victorian age was one of great and often bewildering change for ordinary people, and though the pictures evoke an impression of slower times, life was as busy and hectic as it is today.

We are fortunate that Frith was a photographer of the people, dedicated to recording the minutiae of everyday life. For it is this sheer wealth of visual data, the painstaking chronicle of changes in dress, transport, street layouts, buildings, housing, engineering and landscape that captivates us so much today. His remarkable images offer us a powerful link with the past and with the lives of our ancestors.

## TODAY'S TECHNOLOGY

Computers have now made it possible for Frith's many thousands of images to be accessed almost instantly. In the Frith archive today, each photograph is carefully 'digitised' then stored on a CD Rom. Frith archivists can locate a single photograph amongst thousands within seconds. Views can be catalogued and sorted under a variety of categories of place and content to the immediate benefit of researchers. Inexpensive reference prints can be created for them at the touch of a mouse button, and a wide range of books and other printed materials assembled and published for a wider, more general readership - in the next twelve months over a hundred Frith local history titles will be published! The

**See Frith at www. francisfrith.co.uk**

day-to-day workings of the archive are very different from how they were in Francis Frith's time: imagine the herculean task of sorting through eleven tons of glass negatives as Frith had to do to locate a particular sequence of pictures! Yet the archive still prides itself on maintaining the same high standards of excellence laid down by Francis Frith, including the painstaking cataloguing and indexing of every view.

It is curious to reflect on how the internet now allows researchers in America and elsewhere greater instant access to the archive than Frith himself ever enjoyed. Many thousands of individual views can be called up on screen within seconds on one of the Frith internet sites, enabling people living continents away to revisit the streets of their ancestral home town, or view places in Britain where they have enjoyed holidays. Many overseas researchers welcome the chance to view special theme selections, such as transport, sports, costume and ancient monuments.

We are certain that Francis Frith would have heartily approved of these modern developments, for he himself was always working at the very limits of Victorian photographic technology.

## THE VALUE OF THE ARCHIVE TODAY

Because of the benefits brought by the computer, Frith's images are increasingly studied by social historians, by researchers into genealogy and ancestory, by architects, town planners, and by teachers and schoolchildren involved in local history projects. In addition, the archive offers every one of us a unique opportunity to examine the places where we and our families have lived and worked down the years. Immensely successful in Frith's own era, the archive is now, a century and more on, entering a new phase of popularity.

## THE PAST IN TUNE WITH THE FUTURE

Historians consider the Francis Frith Collection to be of prime national importance. It is the only archive of its kind remaining in private ownership and has been valued at a million pounds. However, this figure is now rapidly increasing as digital technology enables more and more people around the world to enjoy its benefits.

Francis Frith's archive is now housed in an historic timber barn in the beautiful village of Teffont in Wiltshire. Its founder would not recognize the archive office as it is today. In place of the many thousands of dusty boxes containing glass plate negatives and an all-pervading odour of photographic chemicals, there are now ranks of computer screens. He would be amazed to watch his images travelling round the world at unimaginable speeds through network and internet lines.

The archive's future is both bright and exciting. Francis Frith, with his unshakeable belief in making photographs available to the greatest number of people, would undoubtedly approve of what is being done today with his lifetime's work. His photographs, depicting our shared past, are now bringing pleasure and enlightenment to millions around the world a century and more after his death.

# SURREY – *An Introduction*

Surrey's beautiful landscape and picturesque towns and villages have been praised and loved for generations. During Queen Victoria's reign many artists and writers flocked there to live and work in the peaceful countryside, and in those days Surrey certainly seemed a world away from London. Yet, for centuries, this most loved of the Home Counties has been within London's sphere. In recent years changes to rural Surrey, for so long imperceptible, have increased inexorably; today, many of the quaint 'old fashioned' aspects of the county beloved of the writers and artists and photographed by Frith & Co have been crowded out.

Surrey today is frequently considered a suburban county, a neat garden-and-parkland setting for wealthy houses, rather than real countryside This is scarcely fair: Surrey is still primarily a land of working farms - but it is true that London has been a greedy neighbour. The 1889 London Government Act that created the new county of London captured part of Surrey and annexed the south bank of the River Thames - the bank still lovingly referred to by those who ply the river as 'the Surrey side'. Further incursions took place in 1965 and again in 1974, abolishing the old county of Middlesex (except as a postal district!) so that Staines, on the north bank of the Thames, became a Surrey town.

That Surrey retains a rural aspect is largely owing to the 'Green Belt' policy, which checks the physical expansion of London, and to the continued efforts of those who wish to preserve the landscape. Even so, there are seemingly insatiable demands for land both for housing and for roads. Over the last hundred and fifty years the old towns have expanded onto erstwhile fields and meadows, while new roads, including the M25, the M3 and the M23, have cut through the beauties of Surrey's landscape. During these years of change, Frith and Co, from their Surrey headquarters in Reigate, were very well placed to record the county in detail.

Surrey's landscape is extremely varied, and therein lies much of the county's magic. The 'Surrey Hills' is an affectionate nickname, including the uplands of the intricate greensand country and the rolling chalklands of the North Downs. Here are such renowned beauty spots as Leith Hill and Box Hill, beloved alike by generations of picnickers and walkers. Rivers have cut deep, verdant vales through the high chalkland. This is good farming country, under the plough and grazed by herds and flocks for generations. The short, sweet turf of the North Downs around Banstead was known for splendid sheep. The hills at Banstead have another claim to fame: horses have raced here since the early 17th century, and Epsom racecourse came to prominence in 1789 when the Earl of Derby introduced the Oaks Stakes for fillies.

close to the Hampshire border and the citadels of Aldershot and Camberley.

The high heaths continue into the south west around Hindhead and Haslemere, where holidaymakers flock to gaze at the splendid valley of the Devil's Punchbowl. To the south east, where it borders Sussex and Kent, Surrey lies in the clay Weald, that great expanse which glimmers into the distance in the views from the Surrey Hills.

Today Surrey has lost much of her tradi-

The Derby, for colts, was introduced in 1790. The opening of the Wells at Epsom - where the fashionable came to take the waters rich in Epsom Salts - itself brought more riders to the Downs.

North west Surrey is of a quite different aspect, an upland region of sandy heaths and clumps of pines. Bagshot Heath in days gone by was the haunt of highwaymen, and now the whole area is much given over to the army, which moved into north west Surrey during Victorian times, taking over the heathland that was unprofitable to the farmer and at that time but sparsely populated. You are never far from the military in west Surrey,

tional northern boundary along the Thames, but it still lays claim to sufficient of England's 'Royal River', through Staines and Chertsey, Walton and Weybridge, for this old watery highway to be an integral part of the county.

Surrey's history is long. Guildford High Street lies along the important prehistoric routeway that runs along the chalk hills from Hampshire to Canterbury. This route was used by chert and flint traders of Neolithic times, and has continued in use through the passing ages. It is a living part of Surrey's past.

The county came by its name during Saxon times. Following the Norman Conquest several castles were built, including

Reigate, Guildford and Farnham. The two hundred and fifty years or so following the Battle of Hastings saw the growth of many of Surrey's market towns, allowing Guildford to rise to its pre-eminent position. The Normans were god-fearing men who built and rebuilt churches on a grand scale, including St Mary's at Guildford. Monasteries were also founded, but not many, though Waverley Abbey, founded in 1128, was the first house of Cistercians in England. The Dominican friary at Guildford was founded by Eleanor of Provence, widow of Henry III, in memory of her little grandson, Prince Henry, who died at Guildford in 1274. The great Benedictine Chertsey Abbey, founded in AD666 and burnt by the Danes in AD872, had been recolonised in the 10th century. Most of Surrey had been included in the Diocese of Winchester ever since its foundation in the 7th century, and the Bishop's Palace - the castle - at Farnham was built in Norman times. It is now the seat of the Bishop of Guildford.

In 1216 Farnham Castle, along with Reigate and Guildford castles, fell to the French Dauphin. This was during the Barons' War with King John, a year after he had signed the Magna Carta in the Surrey meadow of Runnymede. The crown prince of France was called across the channel by the barons, incensed that the king had failed to comply with the charter's conditions.

The Tudor period was of great importance in the history of Surrey. This was the first time in the county's history that it came into favour as an out-of-town resort. Henry VII rebuilt Sheen Palace and christened it 'Richmond' - he had been Duke of Richmond prior to winning the crown. Henry VIII started the building of Nonsuch, that now-vanished palace that was to be a favourite with Queen Elizabeth, who also stayed at Oatlands, Weybridge, another of Henry VIII's creations. Wealthy politicians, lawyers and merchants followed suit and built themselves grand mansions in the county, frequently using wealth redistributed from religious houses. Many farmhouses and cottages in Surrey were built during Tudor times, their facades later rendered or clad in hung tiles so that their half-

timbered construction is not at first apparent. Some of these appear in the old photographs of this book.

During the Civil War Surrey had strong Parliamentarian leanings. None the less, Farnham Castle changed hands several times. The last serious engagement of the war took place in Surrey in 1648, when a small Royalist army was routed on Surbiton Common by a superior Parliamentary force.

Industry was important in Surrey in the centuries before the Industrial Revolution when water mills on the main rivers (Mole, Wandle, Tillingbourne and Wey) provided power for the manufacture of cloth, paper, iron, brass and gunpowder. Some of the mills survived the Industrial Revolution as flour/grist mills, and were photographed by Frith before their final dereliction and demolition. Happily, some survive to this day.

The handiwork of the canal era is written large in Surrey, for the first British attempt to improve a river for navigation took place in the county. In 1653 Sir Richard Weston of Sutton Place obtained an Act of Parliament to make the River Wey navigable from Guildford to the Thames, so that Wealden oak could be transported downstream. In 1760 the navigation was extended upstream to Godalming, and the canal also shipped meal and corn as well as paper and gunpowder. The Basingstoke Canal, with its flight of locks at Deepcut, was completed in 1794. Deepcut, known for its army camp, is named after the 70ft deep 1,000 yd long cutting that carries the canal across the high heathland of west Surrey. Other canals followed: the Surrey Canal (1801) and the Wey and Arun Junction Canal (1813).

The era of laden barges plying the waterways and of stagecoaches jolting over miles of turnpiked roads gave way to the railway era, though right up till 1905 there were attempts to revive the coaching business. The London to Greenwich railway line opened in 1838, swiftly followed by the Croydon railway in 1839. Soon 'railway towns' were springing up across the woods, fields and heaths of Surrey: Redhill, Woking, and Surbiton. And where the towns were not entirely new creations, the older centres started to grow at a far greater pace than they did in the turnpike era. The speculative builder moved in. So too did former London residents, either as holiday makers or as new denizens of Surrey, both businessmen who could commute by train and artists and writers. These included George Meredith, William and Helen Allingham and G F Watts, who found in its quiet peace a sense of beauty to enable them to fulfil their callings.

After the First World War the roads, revitalised by the motor car, brought trippers and another wave of new-style residents, with their London ideas of what the countryside should be. The narrow streets of Surrey's towns, built for different traffic, were choked by cars as early as the late 1920s; thus the by-pass was born, beginning with the Guildford and Godalming bypass, completed in 1934. It was but a short step to the motorways of today, which have carved up some of Surrey's loveliest landscape - Gatton Bottom, for example - and brought with them not only air pollution but shattering noise.

The post-war years have seen an acceleration of change. The intimate character of many a Surrey townscape has been destroyed, sometimes with the wholesale sweeping away of the past in favour of a future of concrete and glass. Surrey's towns and villages, in the pre mass-production era, each had their own special face, sometimes quirky, sometimes sober and dignified, but never 'faceless'. Numerous examples of this individuality are seen in these photographs, including Leatherhead's jaunty clock tower-cum-firestation set awkwardly at the crossroads, and Godalming's 'pepperpot' market house - fortunately still standing - and its tortuously twisting narrow streets. There was Dorking's High Street of rather unremarkable buildings jostling together towards the prospect of Box Hill, to afford a most pleasing and unforgettable vista. Surrey's most famous town view is jealously guarded and protected: you can still look down the steep slope of Guildford High Street with its projecting clock towards the green mass of Guildown on the opposite side of the Wey valley. The streets of Farnham are in certain respects unchanged. Epsom still has its clock tower, Reigate still has its old town hall and Haslemere still has its wide main street.

Surrey's townscapes, particularly as seen in these old photographs, owed much to the Georgian era. If this is true of Farnham even today, it was also once true of Dorking, and of Guildford beyond its renowned High Street. An important element of any townscape is its inns. Many in Surrey date from those days when travel was truly a 'travail' along uncertain roads. Some of these Surrey inns predate the coaching era by many centuries - such as the White Hart in Bletchingly and the White Horse in Dorking, both pictured here before the motor-car era. Other old inns pictured here have vanished from the face of the earth, like Guildford's renowned Red Lion.

The photographs have been grouped into five chapters, with towns and villages so arranged as to produce a nostalgic touring guide. Starting at Guildford, the county town, we set out in imagination along the old roads linking the old settlements. We pass through a Surrey much of which has passed away, with its watermills, its elegant High Streets, its waterways and its quaint cottages. This echo of tangible things that have vanished - many of them gone since the Second World War - is surely an eloquent plea that Surrey needs protection, that we have lost too much of value since Frith's photographers took their pictures. It is up to us whether we listen to that plea.

**GUILDFORD, FRIARY STREET 1904** 51857

A scene that has been swallowed up in the creation of the new road system and the Friary Shopping Centre on the site of the Dominican Friary. The buildings along this ancient lane were demolished prior to 1969, and it is now a modern pedestrianised area.

**GUILDFORD, HIGH STREET 1895** 35060a
This classic view looks west down High Street
to the Wey valley and beyond to Guildown
(The Mount). Over one hundred years' later,
Guildown still closes this view, with the
famous clock of 1683 jutting out from the
Elizabethan Guildhall. The clock was made
by London clockmaker John Aylward.

**GUILDFORD, HIGH STREET 1903** 50871

A picture taken eight years later than No 35060A, and lower down the High Street towards the river. The Ford of Guildford was here, and still existed until 1760 when the channel was deepened for navigation. St Nicolas church, built 1874-6, stands on the opposite side of the river.

**GUILDFORD, MARKET STREET 1904** 51858

Most of Market Street was taken up by the now demolished Red Lion. The hotel was mentioned by that seasoned traveller John Aubrey in the early 17th century, and was a frequent stopping place for Pepys, who particularly enjoyed the garden at the back. The site of the Red Lion was later a Timothy Whites.

## GUILDFORD
### York Road 1904

This photograph is a real period piece - note the old-style perambulator. Here we look along the present A246 to the east of the town, showing the Victorian terraced housing. Note the trees planted right at the edge of the kerb.

◆

## GUILDFORD
### The Castle 1895

The ruinous 70ft high 12th century keep, all that remains of Henry III's favourite palace. It was the only Royal Castle in Surrey; the motte was raised soon after the Norman Conquest. The only action the castle ever saw was in 1216, when it was occupied by the French at the invitation of the Barons rebelling against King John.

**GUILDFORD, YORK ROAD 1904** 51864

**GUILDFORD, THE CASTLE 1895** 35064

**GUILDFORD, THE CASTLE GROUNDS FISH POND 1906** 54155

**GUILDFORD**

*The Castle Grounds Fish Pond 1906*

The Castle grounds include the 200-year old bowling green, and were laid out as a pleasure garden when Guildford Corporation bought the Castle in the 1880s. The three little Edwardian girls seem like a triple echo of 'Alice in Wonderland', whose creator, Lewis Carroll, spent many vacations with his sisters at Guildford and died here in 1898.

◆

**GUILDFORD**

*St Catherine's Ferry 1895*

Ferry Lane, on the so-called Pilgrims' Way, runs down to the River Wey and the site of the former ferry, which was inaugurated prior to 1377. The ferry ran for the last time in 1964, but the present footbridge was not built until 1985, linking again the two halves of the North Downs Way.

**GUILDFORD, ST CATHERINE'S FERRY 1895** 35620

**GUILDFORD, FROM PEWLEY HILL 1895** 35055

This view looks towards a naked Stag Hill, now crowned by Guildford Cathedral and flanked by the University of Surrey. The Cathedral was begun in 1936 and completed in 1961. St Nicolas' church is in the middle distance. The name Pewley Hill derives from the de-la-Puille family, who owned the land in the 13th century.

**FARNCOMBE, THE RIVER c1955** F10002

The Godalming Navigation, the extension of the Wey Navigation added in 1760-2, can be explored from Farncombe Boat House either by boat or by walking along the agreeable towpath. The boathouse is one of the last in England where you can hire a punt.

**FARNCOMBE, HIGH STREET 1905** 53234a
Now virtually part of the sprawl of Godalming, this picture shows Farncombe when it was still a village beside the River Wey. It is separated from Godalming by the watermeadows known as 'lammas lands', grazed by cattle for centuries.

**GODALMING, HIGH STREET 1903** 49197
Godalming was initially an industrial town, noted for its cloth making. On the left of the cobbled High Street, notably devoid of any traffic, is Edward's Drug Store, which later passed to Boots. The building, in brick and stone, dates from the late 17th century.

**GODALMING, HIGH STREET 1895** 36153
Here we see a cobbled High Street in the sunlight of one of the last years of the 19th century. There is not a vehicle in sight. On the left is a butcher's shop, whilst a horse waits patiently. On the right is the Great George Inn.

**GODALMING, THE MUNICIPAL BUILDINGS 1908** 59949

A view of Borough Hall, Bride Street. This is a rather dull building built by J H Norris, the Borough Surveyor, in 1906. The poster advertises a military tattoo, whilst on the extreme right is a cycle shop.

**GODALMING, BOARDEN BRIDGE 1906** 54688

Looking south across the River Wey, with a group of children posing for the photographer in front of the wooden Boarden Bridge, the centuries-old crossing point. Behind is the brick Borough Bridge of 1870, nicknamed 'Lunatic Bridge' because of its unnecessarily high arches. In the background is the medieval church of St Peter and St Paul, with its 13th-century lead spire - rare in Surrey.

**GODALMING, THE MARKET HOUSE 1903** 49265
Known affectionately as 'The Pepperpot', Godalming's attractive market house of 1814 stands at the junction of three streets in central Godalming. From early Victorian times onwards the arcaded ground floor was bricked up and used as lumber room and public convenience, as this photograph shows. The arcade was reopened in 1955.

**GODALMING, FROM NEW WAY 1907** 57510
A view of industrial Godalming from just above the railway line. In the right foreground is a mill pond on a tributary valley. Godalming was well known for its manufacture of cloth, and the mill with its tall chimney is a reminder of this industrial heritage.

**GODALMING**
*Boating on the River Wey 1908*
A tranquil scene from a vanished summer: ladies are punting on the meadow-fringed river. With the closure of the Wey and Arun canal almost fifty years earlier, this stretch of the river saw little traffic.

**GODALMING**
*Charterhouse 1927*
The school dominates the skyline above Godalming. In 1872, it moved here from Charterhouse Square, London, where it had existed since its foundation in 1611. The main gothic-style buildings with their towers were designed by Philip Hardwick. Thackeray, John Wesley and Vaughan Williams were all educated here.

GODALMING, BOATING ON THE RIVER WEY 1908  59957

GODALMING, CHARTERHOUSE 1927  79351

**CRANLEIGH, ROWLANDS CORNER 1904**  51303

Here we see Cranleigh's old village hall at Rowlands Corner, with its attendant shops. It is now the British Legion building, and a new 'village' hall has been built in the centre of town. Cranleigh (formerly Cranley) was once a centre of the Wealden iron industry, but has grown quickly in the 20th century.

**CRANLEIGH, THE POND 1906**  56763

Village boys stand at the edge of the pond in Horseshoe Lane, which was used for washing carts - note the floating board. The buildings behind comprise Brown's butcher's shop and slaughter house, long since adapted to domestic uses.

**CRANLEIGH, THE STATION 1908** 59697
This is a long-vanished scene. A train approaches the down platform of this station on the Horsham to Guildford Railway, which opened in 1865 and is long since closed. There were five stations, Bramley, Cranleigh, Baynards, Rudgwick and Slinfold.

**DORKING, A BACKWATER 1913** 65212
An enchanting corner of old Dorking: the photographer has captured a moment with two people standing in their respective doorways, and a cat sitting on the left looking at the bearded man. Note the cobble stones, the pot plants, the juxtaposition of the roof-lines - and the Victorian hung tiles on the right.

**DORKING, MILTON COURT 1906** 54675
This house stands a mile or so west of Dorking, and dates from about 1610, with alterations from about 1864 when the roofline was changed. The translator of Euripedes, Jeremiah Markland, died here. The house still stands.

**DORKING, DEEPDENE 1891** 29567
A fine view of a house whose gardens were compared by John Aubrey with 'the kingdom of heaven'. It was rebuilt by the art collector Thomas Hope who had inherited it in 1807, and Disraeli wrote most of 'Coningsby' here in 1844. The house was used by the Railways in the Second World War, but was demolished in 1968.

**DORKING, HIGH STREET 1905** 53334
Dorking's architectural heritage has been decimated since the Second World War. This view of the High Street has changed out of all recognition - though the 15th-century White Horse, a famous coaching inn in the centre of the picture, still stands, and the view is still terminated by the green baulk of Box Hill.

**DORKING, SOUTH STREET 1907** 57635

## DORKING
### *South Street 1907*

South Street has been less spoiled than other streets in Dorking, and many of its old buildings remain. This picture looks towards the parish church of St Martin, with its 210ft high spire, still the town's dominant feature today. The spire was added to the 19th-century church in 1874 in memory of Bishop Wilberforce.

◆

## DORKING
### *The Mill 1903*

Castle Mill stands on the River Mole and was recorded in Domesday. It was always a corn mill, and was enlarged in the 1830s with four pairs of stones, storerooms and other outbuildings. Partially destroyed by fire in 1933, it stopped production in 1952 and is now a private house.

**DORKING, THE MILL 1903** 50967

**DORKING, THE FORT TEA GARDENS c1955** D45088

A marvellous view of the once bustling scene at the tea rooms near the summit of Box Hill, close to the Monument. The Old Fort itself was built against the French. It was derelict but is being restored.

**WESTCOTT, THE VILLAGE SIGN 1922** 71742

Now on the A25, this village lies between the north downs and the Leith Hill sandstone range. This unusual village sign, signpost, direction indicator and dovecote, is situated on the triangular shaped central green.

**WESTCOTT, THE ROOKERY 1904** 52192
The now-demolished birthplace of the economist Thomas Malthus, who prophesised the huge growth in human population and the need for birth control. His 'Essay on the Principle of Population' (1798) was written here. The children seem blissfully unaware.

**WESTCOTT, THE ROOKERY MILL HOUSE 1933** 85494
Yet another vanished Surrey watermill, testimony to a virtually forgotten source of power. This mill stood on the Pippbroook, a tributary of the Mole, but has now been demolished. It was one of six mills on the little Pippbrook alone. The next mill downstream was at Westcott itself.

**GOMSHALL, THE MILL 1904** 51810
Little girls pose for the cameraman on the ford at the Tillingbourne. 'Gomeselle' was mentioned in Domesday, at which time a mill already existed at the site. Gomshall tanneries were known world-wide, but were taken over and closed in 1988.

EAST HORSLEY, THE TOWERS c1955   H120013

**EAST HORSLEY**
*The Towers c1955*
This mock-Tudor Gothic mansion can be glimpsed from the road. It was for many years the offices of the electricity board and had been created by Lord Lovelace who bought it in 1840. Part of the tower dates from his rebuilding from 1858.

◆

**CLANDON**
*The Village Shop 1911*
A marvellous set piece, showing East Clandon Post Office. The man posing proudly for the camera outside the shop is Mr Smith himself. A lady is posting a letter, with her dog sitting obediently. The postman is visible with his bicycle on the far right.

CLANDON, THE VILLAGE SHOP 1911   63147X

**CLANDON, CLANDON ALEXANDRA HOSPITAL 1913** 65232
The country branch of the Queen Alexandra Nursing Home for Children with Hip Disease was at East Clandon.
In fine weather the children were allowed onto the veranda in their cots, or if not bedridden, to sit and read.
They were known for waving happily to passers-by.

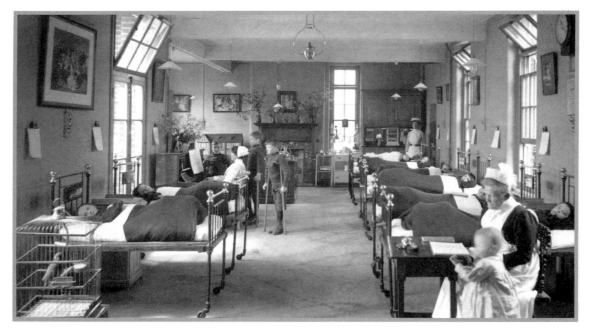

**CLANDON, CLANDON ALEXANDRA HOSPITAL 1913** 65233
The atmosphere of this photograph is almost unbearably tragic, but is relieved by a nurse playing the piano in
the background, whilst boys on crutches sing. A child on the right has a reading lesson and a caged parrot is in
the left foreground.

**REIGATE, VANDERBILT'S COACH VENTURE 1886** 18968B

After the opening of the railway from London to Brighton in 1841, the coaching era came quickly to a close. However, towards the end of the 19th century, coaching was revived as a romantic alternative to the age of steam, and here is one such revival on the Brighton Road outside Reigate.

**REIGATE, THE CASTLE GROUNDS 1915** 67779

Reigate Castle has vanished completely, but its 11th-century motte is now a rose garden known as Castle Grounds. The little gatehouse is a folly built in 1777, while the Baron's Caves which lie beneath were used as a magazine during the First World War.

### REIGATE
#### *Rice Bridge on the Mole 1886*

A group, thought to be part of a 'walking party', pose rather self-consciously on the two-arched bridge over the River Mole. This stands across the fields some two miles to the south west of Reigate.

### REIGATE
#### *A Shopping Excursion 1906*

This wonderful scene is taken just off the High Street. It shows a charming group of fashionable children, out shopping with their mother in Edwardian days. This family scene contrasts with the workaday scene of the carts in the middle distance.

REIGATE, RICE BRIDGE ON THE MOLE 1886   18821

REIGATE, A SHOPPING EXCURSION 1906   54148V

REIGATE, THE TOWN HALL AND MARKET PLACE 1921 70937
In the centre of the town is the 1728 brick-built Old Town
Hall, with an open arcaded ground floor. The slate lantern,
part of the adjoining clock tower, dates from 1811, and
gives the whole structure a jaunty air. The scene is familiar
today, although the traffic has changed.

**REIGATE, BELL STREET 1936** 87306
Bell Street runs south from the main cross roads. The Ancient House Bookshop on the right hand side is little changed today, although the wonderful metal sign for Reigate Garage has now disappeared. On the left is Reigate Park. Today there is substantially more traffic.

**REIGATE, WRAY COMMON WINDMILL 1907** 59254
This tower mill still stands, though it is now a private house and has lost its sails. It was built in 1824 of tarred brick, and is situated on the rough open space of Wray Common between Reigate and its neighbour Redhill.

### EARLSWOOD
#### *A Motor 'Bus 1919*

A fine view of an early motorised 'bus, heading through Earlswood on its way to Horley, just after the First World War. Earlswood is known for its common and its two recreational ponds separated by a wooden footbridge.

### EARLSWOOD
#### *New Pond 1922*

Earlswood Lakes are on Earlswood Common, south of Redhill, and really in the clay Weald. The ponds lie across the road from New Pond Farm, where today there is a nature reserve. Note the array of hats among the spectators on the left.

EARLSWOOD, A MOTOR 'BUS 1919   68890X

EARLSWOOD, NEW POND 1922   71834

**EARLSWOOD, NEW POND 1922** 71835

A wonderful evocative scene of people enjoying themselves on the pond; note in particular the boat with a canopy. New Pond was dug in the 14th century (Upper Pond is an old brick pit) and was once a popular bathing place. It is now stocked with fish and bathing is prohibited.

**SALFORDS, THE MONOTYPE WORKS 1911** 63427

Employees are leaving the Monotype factory. Many travellers on the Brighton line will remember the Monotype name, as it was advertised along the factory buildings which backed on to the railway line. Monotype came to Salfords in 1901, and made all kinds of hot metal castings for the printing trade.

**BETCHWORTH, THE VILLAGE AND THE CHURCH c1939** B76001
An exquisite snow scene looking towards the mainly 13th-century St Michael's Church, which was much altered in the 19th century when the Norman tower was re-positioned half-way along the south aisle. The old black-painted tithe barn stands on the right.

**BETCHWORTH, THE CHALK PIT 1907** 57274
Not only lime but also some building stone was formerly quarried in the huge Betchworth chalk pit. It had its own narrow gauge railway, which is visible here. The quarry once belonged to Sir Benjamin Brodie, Royal surgeon to Queen Victoria and president of the Royal College of Surgeons.

**BETCHWORTH, FROM THE CHURCH 1900** 45009

Modern buildings have crowded in along the northern part of Betchworth's long village street, but the line of the North Downs and the big chalk pit remain much the same, although the downs are far more wooded.

**LEATHERHEAD, THE CLOCK TOWER 1888** 21343

The quaint clock-tower has gone in the rebuilding that has overtaken Leatherhead; it used to stand atop the old fire station. This view is looking down Gravel Hill. This is a quiet mid-afternoon picture, deserted save for workmen re-fitting the shopfront to the post office on the left.

**LEATHERHEAD**
*Bridge Street 1899*
Bridge Street slopes down to the river Mole and the 14-arch bridge of 1782. Beside the bridge on the right of the picture is the Running Horse, a 16th-century inn which features in John Skelton's 'Tunning of Elinor Rumming', a rampant piece of doggerel about an alewife.

◆

**LEATHERHEAD**
*The Old Mill 1906*
Leatherhead's mill pond was famous in its day for its depth and clarity. In this photograph the weatherboarded old mill totters towards decay, but times for swimming in the pond are advertised and a butcher's cart poses for the picture.

LEATHERHEAD, BRIDGE STREET 1899 43514

LEATHERHEAD, THE OLD MILL 1906 54882

**LEATHERHEAD, NORTH STREET 1906** 54878
New buildings and modern traffic have altered this scene almost beyond recognition. Note on the left Hartshorn the Butcher, purveyor to the Duke of Connaught. Note the fire station and post office also seen in picture 21343.

**LEATHERHEAD, PLOUGHING 1925** 78064A

### LEATHERHEAD
*Ploughing 1925*

This was once a familiar sight in the farming lands of Surrey: great horses slowly pacing across the autumnal landscape with the ploughman gripping the handles to plough a straight furrow, turning the old grey earth to brown.

### LEATHERHEAD
*On the Mole 1902*

A bowler-hatted gentleman contemplates this tranquil river scene looking towards the gracious arches of the viaduct that carries the railway to Effingham junction. Today the view through the railway arches is one of industrial buildings, with a playing field at the river's edge.

**LEATHERHEAD, ON THE MOLE 1902** 48876

## ASHSTEAD
### *The Swimming Pool 1929*

Samuel Pepys knew Ashtead as a boy, and in later years called it 'my old place of delight'. Certainly this view suggests delight - with swimmers poised on the diving boards amid the tree-fringed beauty of Ashtead's outdoor pool.

◆

## EPSOM
### *High Street 1907*

A nostalgic view of a quiet Epsom High Street, with horse-drawn traffic and pedestrians only - plus a few dogs - and a gas lamp standard. An old watch tower used to stand on the site of the Clock Tower of 1854, close to a large pond, which was infilled when the tower was built.

ASHSTEAD, THE SWIMMING POOL 1929  82278

EPSOM, HIGH STREET 1907  58595

**EPSOM, HIGH STREET 1924** 75368

This is the main cross roads in central Epsom, High Street and Waterloo Street, and is gloriously uncluttered in this period view. The 17th-century inn, the Spread Eagle, much altered in the 19th century, was originally a favourite with visitors to Epsom Spa - and still caters for visitors to the famous races.

**EPSOM, HIGH STREET AND THE CLOCK TOWER c1955** E37004

A final view of Epsom town, with its wide High Street and only a little traffic. The clock tower, with public lavatories at its base, was about 100 years old when this picture was taken. The tower commemorates the Public Health Act of 1848.

**EPSOM, WOODCOTE PARK 1927** 79671

Formerly Epsom's grandest house, Woodcote Park was bought by the RAC in 1911. It is seen here in its former glory, for it was burned down in 1934; it has since been rebuilt in brick - a copy of the stone original.

**EPSOM, WOODCOTE PARK 1917** 68005

Woodcote Park was commandeered by the War Office in 1915, and Humphreys of Knightsbridge were contracted to build not only huts but also a chapel and a splendid recreation room. It stands on the far right of this photograph, which gives a general view of the barracks.

**EPSOM, DERBY DAY 1927** E37305
All those hats! There is not a bare head
to be seen in this view, which looks
towards the old grandstand - new the
year this picture was taken. It
accommodated 20,000 people,
compared with the 6,000 of the 1830
grandstand. And an estimated 512,000
people watched the race.

**EPSOM, THE START OF THE DERBY 1927** E37001
Off they go! This famous race was won this year by Frank Curzon's 'Call Boy'. Important visitors to the 1927 Derby included members of the Royal Family and Captain Lindbergh, hero of trans-Atlantic flight.

**EWELL, RUXLEY SPLASH 1907** 58600
A marvellously posed picture of the Ruxley watersplash, at Ewell on the Hogsmill River. It was situated in Ruxley Lane, now the B284. Note the old footbridge and causeway to the left of the picture, now replaced by a bridge.

**EWELL**
*The Pond 1903*
The pond is in central Ewell; the wall separates it from the grounds of Bourne Hall on the right. Note the top-hatted driver of the horse conveyance in the centre of the picture, and the horse in the pond on the left.

**EWELL**
*The Spring Hotel and the Coach 1924*
This picture was taken at the junction of London Road and Kingston Road. The coach appears to be a revival of the great days of the coach era when many such 'equipages' used to pass through here. The Spring Hotel is an old established inn.

EWELL, THE POND 1903 50514

EWELL, THE SPRING HOTEL AND THE COACH 1924 75486

**EWELL, NONSUCH PARK ENTRANCE c1955** E45034
This building was designed by Sir Jeffrey Wyatville and built in 1802-6; only its name recalls Henry VIII's now vanished palace. It was sold in 1937 to London and Surrey County Councils, following the death of the last member of the Farmer family, who had lived there for many years.

**RIDDLESDOWN, THE VIADUCT 1907** 57469
An interesting view of the railway viaduct, which carried the Croydon to Oxted line through Riddlesdown quarry. The tops of lime kilns can be seen poking out in the gap on the right.

**CATERHAM, CHURCH HILL 1903** 50970

The carter poses for this photograph, whilst a family are out for a walk on the pavement. The road has not changed, but the chalet-style house has gone, replaced by luxury flats, and there are now houses to the right.

**CATERHAM, GENERAL VIEW 1925** 78126

A fine prospect of Caterham, taken looking west from the steep scarp slope of the north downs above Crescent Road. The hilly and wooded nature of the landscape is clearly seen, and the view is surprisingly little changed today.

**CATERHAM, A MOTOR 'BUS 1925** 78135V
The 'bus takes pride of place in this bustling High Street scene from the 1920s. The view, taken from what is now a roundabout looking towards London, is surprisingly little changed. There is now a restaurant on the extreme right, but the Surrey Arms behind the bus is still there.

**CATERHAM, THE BARRACKS C1955** C49032

A scene that is now no more: the barracks stood on Caterham Hill, where the sentry is standing guard at the entrance. The Barracks was closed in the 1990s, and the buildings are being demolished and the site redeveloped.

**CATERHAM, PEPPER ALLEY 1907** 57978

A finely-composed scene, reflecting the verdant and rural side of this former military town. The view shows one of the wooded and sloping pathways that abound on the steep sides of the North Downs.

**TANDRIDGE, THE VILLAGE 1907** 57972a
This unusual picture presumably shows a Frith photographer at work. The dapper photographer has clearly caught the attention of the old ladies at the gate of the cottage. His plate glass camera looks surprisingly compact for Edwardian times, a far cry from the heavy studio cameras prevalent at the time.

**GODSTONE, IVY MILL 1898** 42753
A superb view epitomising the rural nature of Surrey before the First World War. Ivy Mill, on the left, with the pond embankment behind, was mentioned in Domesday and was always an important corn-milling site. Ivy House on the right dates from 1698.

**BLETCHINGLEY, THE VILLAGE 1905** 53206
This is the wide High Street along the A25, where once a market was held; now it is all too often choked with traffic. The White Harte was built in the 16th century and refronted in the 18th century.

**BLETCHINGLEY, THE ALMSHOUSES 1907** 57500

These 19th-century almshouses stand in Bletchingley High Street. Bletchingley became a borough in the early 13th century and returned two MPs until the 1832 Reform Act.

**BLETCHINGLEY, THE VILLAGE 1886** 18980

Cobbles, brick, timber and tile - an enchanting corner of Bletchingley over one hundred years ago. This view is of Middle Row of Church Walk, a cobbled alley which leads to the parish church at the east, and has little changed today. Note the attractive tile-hung overhangs.

**WOKING, CHERTSEY ROAD 1898** 42025

This railway town was some two miles north of the original village of Old Woking. The London to Southampton railway arrived in 1838, and 'new' Woking began to develop. The town has mushroomed in size and been redeveloped since this picture was taken, and few of the Victorian buildings survive.

**WOKING, CHERTSEY ROAD c1955** W122028

Almost sixty years after photograph No 42025 was taken, Frith's photographers returned to take a further view down Chertsey Road. The contrast between the two scenes is remarkable, chiefly because of the cars which now throng the road; the contrast with the scene today is even greater.

**WOKING, MAYBURY ROAD 1902** 48347
A view of the parade of shops that once graced this elegant road. Today, Maybury is the centre of a large Muslim community, centred on the Shah Jehan Mosque, the oldest mosque in Britain, which was built in 1889, and was thus thirteen years old when this picture was taken.

**WOKING, OLD BANK 1901** 46337

Buildings such as Woking's fine, if somewhat dull, Old Bank had no place in the exciting, post-war redeveloped Woking. Note the workmen and the long ladders up the buildings on the left, and the semaphore signals on the railway in the right distance.

**WOKING, CHOBHAM ROAD 1902** 48346

A final view of Woking and its parades of shops, this time on the Chobham Road. There seem few customers out and about, and the only traffic on the road is to be seen in the far distance. Note the drug stores on the right with the gigantic pestle and mortar symbol on the roofline.

### DEEPCUT CAMP
**The Garrison Church 1906**

This large white-painted corrugated iron church sports an 'army green' roof and bell turret. Dedicated to St Barbara, patron saint of warriors, it is open to the public, and was built in 1901. The stained glass windows display regimental badges.

### DEEPCUT CAMP
**The Gun Park 1906**

A view of the ordnance depot of the Royal Army Ordnance Corps. The guns appear to bear more resemblance to those used at Waterloo than to those that would be used eight years later at the outbreak of the Great War. The regimental dog is in the left foreground.

**DEEPCUT CAMP, THE GARRISON CHURCH 1906** 54922

**DEEPCUT CAMP, THE GUN PARK 1906** 55051

**DEEPCUT CAMP, THE RFA JUST OFF CHURCH PARADE 1906** 55050
The Royal Field Artillery pose informally for the camera. In 1906 there was still a great deal of romance attached to soldiering, perhaps because of the long distance travel it involved, and the glamour of action in far-flung corners of the empire.

**DEEPCUT CAMP, THE MARRIED QUARTERS 1906** 55056
The 'romance' of a soldier's life aside, the architecture certainly makes this a somewhat depressing picture. Two rather grim terraces face each other like advancing armies, so that even the children playing happily and the horses pulling the cart with its wicker baskets cannot quite dispel the bleak atmosphere.

**DEEPCUT CAMP, THE RFA AND GENERAL ALDERSON'S HOUSE 1906** 55055

A fine study of a gunnery team standing to attention at Deepcut Camp. To our eyes, the finely crafted wooden wheels belong to an era one hundred years earlier, and appear obsolete when compared to the type of warfare that would be waged eight years later.

**BLACKDOWN CAMP, THE 2ND BRIGADE OFFICE 1906** 54929

West Surrey has been army country since 1853, when Queen Victoria reviewed her troops on Chobham Common. Blackdown Camp - now Blackdown Barracks - is at Deepcut on the high heathland north of the Basingstoke Canal. The Barracks is the headquarters of the Royal Army Ordnance Corps.

BLACKDOWN CAMP
*The Parade Ground 1906*
A view of pre-First World War soldiers standing at ease on the parade ground. Perhaps they served in the Boer War; in eight years' time these men would be at war again in the battlefields of Europe.

BLACKDOWN CAMP
*The Garrison and The Institute 1906*
Here we see the brick-built army buildings of this military settlement in Surrey's army quarter on the high heathlands of the north west of the county. The group posing for the picture includes three little girls, presumably soldiers' daughters.

BLACKDOWN CAMP, THE PARADE GROUND 1906  54930

BLACKDOWN CAMP, THE GARRISON AND THE INSTITUTE 1906  54928

**BLACKDOWN CAMP, THE SERGEANTS' MESS 1906** 54927
One of the huts of Blackdown Camp, with a group of soldiers and a bowler-hatted civilian. Traditionally the army had very strong links with the aristocracy and gentry, but by the early years of the 20th century the middle classes had gained a foothold.

**BLACKDOWN CAMP, THE GYM 1906** 54934
This unusual picture shows the interior of one of the army buildings at Blackdown Camp. Instruction is taking place in the bright and well-equipped gym. Looking at first sight deceptively like a fencing lesson, the two recruits are in fact being taught the art of bayoneting.

FRIMLEY, THE OLD WINDMILL 1906 54908

### FRIMLEY
### *The Old Windmill 1906*
This old tower windmill is on Old Windmill Hill between Blackdown Barracks and Elizabeth Barracks in Deepcut and Pirbright Camps. Today it is amid the rifle ranges and military control of high, heathy west Surrey.

### FRIMLEY
### *The Lock 1906*
A peaceful view of Frimley Lock, the last of the Deepcut locks flight, which total 14 in all. The Basingstoke canal of 1794 linked the Wey and Godalming Navigation (the River Wey) with Basingstoke. It declined after 1838 and the coming of the railway, and became derelict until it was restored after 1973.

FRIMLEY, THE LOCK 1906 54914

**FRIMLEY GREEN, THE CANAL AND THE NEW BOATHOUSE 1909** 61829
This view looks north from the old Guildford Road Bridge, with the canal aqueduct across the Waterloo - Basingstoke line in the background. The new wooden boathouse, built in 1906 by A J Harmsworth, stands on the left. The man in the punt is Harmsworth's brother, William, who managed the boathouse.

**CAMBERLEY, HIGH STREET 1901** 46832
Camberley grew up at the gates of the Military Staff College which opened in 1862. It was originally called 'Cambridge Town', but soon changed its name to 'Camberley' to avoid confusion with the university town. Its growth engulfed the earlier military settlement at 'York Town' to the west.

**CAMBERLEY, LONDON ROAD 1909** 61462
A study of cyclists and pedestrians on what is now the A30. London Road acts as a dividing line between Camberley the town and the military area - the town, with its line of shops, is to the right of this picture and the grounds of the Royal Military Academy are to the left.

**CAMBERLEY, LONDON ROAD 1925** 78122
This is the same view as in photograph No 61462, but taken sixteen years later. The gap in the foreground in the 1909 picture has now been replaced with an arcade, and cars are now seen rather than bikes and pedestrians.

**CAMBERLEY, THE STAFF COLLEGE, 1901** 46829

This is a formal portrait of a somewhat overpowering and formal building, which is generally considered to be rather fine. It was designed by Pennethorne and completed in 1862. Prince Albert is said to have caught his fatal chill whilst watching it being built.

**CAMBERLEY, THE ENTRANCE TO SANDHURST MILITARY COLLEGE 1906** 56995

York Town - the older part of Camberley - grew on a grid-pattern from the military set-up when the army moved here from Marlow in 1812. The Neo-Doric lodges on the Basingstoke Road were built by Wyatt in 1807-12.

CAMBERLEY, THE ROYAL MILITARY COLLEGE, SANDHURST 1925
76696

## CAMBERLEY
### The Royal Military College, Sandhurst 1925

Here we see a fine view of the main neo-classical building, which is actually in Berkshire. It seems a peaceful setting for men to learn the art of war. During the days of the British Empire, there was always a war somewhere to which the Sandhurst-trained officers could be despatched.

## BAGSHOT
### High Street 1925

There is little motorised traffic, but several bicycles can be seen in this picture of the High Street in busy Bagshot. The town developed around the Old Portsmouth Road over Bagshot Heath from the early 19th century, and most of the buildings in this picture are Victorian.

BAGSHOT, HIGH STREET 1925  78019

**BAGSHOT, THE VIADUCT 1901** 46850
Children idly watch the photographer - and each other - from either side of the road, and wagons stand under one of the arches in Kemp and Sons' yard. On the extreme left is Peel House, built in 1851 and once the police station.

**BAGSHOT, HIGH CURLY HILL 1903** 50990
High Curly Hill is a noted viewpoint on Bagshot Heath in the Lightwater Country Park, with a marked trail leading to the hilltop. A century ago, this was an area of rhododendron and nursery gardens, several of which survive. The Scots pines were introduced to the area in 1800.

**BAGSHOT, VILLAGE CHILDREN 1903** 50991
This beautifully-composed and peaceful
scene in a little lane shows how much life
had changed in the previous century; it
almost mocks Bagshot's reputation as a
haunt of highwaymen, who preyed on
travellers on the Portsmouth Road.

**BAGSHOT, PENNY HILL PARK 1906** 57177
Gardeners tend the remarkable holly hedge of Penny Hill Park, which grows in places up to 40 feet high. Penny Hill Park was built in 1873, and is now an hotel. It has a beautifully landscaped garden.

**COBHAM, PORTSMOUTH ROAD 1931** 84169
This is an unusual view for the time, showing the old Portsmouth Road, now by-passed and merely the A307. Even then, the road shows signs of traffic congestion. Note the substantial old-fashioned telegraph poles and cables, a once-familiar sight on Britain's trunk roads.

**COBHAM, THE MILL 1919** 68857
Children pose on the reedy banks of the River Mole below the impressive double wheeled mill. It was built in the early 19th century as a corn and grist mill, and was run by the firm Henry Moore and Son when this picture was taken. It fell into disuse, and is now mostly demolished.

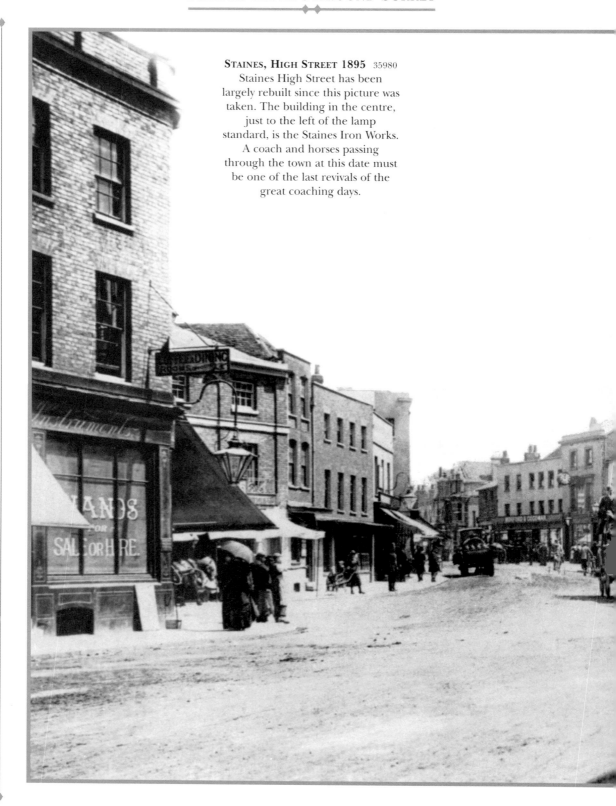

**STAINES, HIGH STREET 1895** 35980
Staines High Street has been largely rebuilt since this picture was taken. The building in the centre, just to the left of the lamp standard, is the Staines Iron Works. A coach and horses passing through the town at this date must be one of the last revivals of the great coaching days.

**STAINES, HIGH STREET 1907** 57995a
This picture gives an excellent view of everyday life in Staines in Edwardian days. Bicycles and horse-drawn vehicles vie for the road in the spacious High Street. A girl and a pram also pose for the camera on the pavement to the right.

**STAINES, THE BRIDGE 1907** 57990

The graceful three-arched bridge over the Thames was rebuilt in 1832 by John and George Rennie, close to the site of the many bridges that have crossed the Thames since the Romans first spanned it. On the opposite side of the bridge is the Swan Hotel. Today, punts are no longer available for hire.

**STAINES, IN THE LOCK 1907** 58000X

A wonderful scene, taken in Edwardian days, of Bell Weir Lock. A conglomeration of craft are passing through the lock on a warm summer's day, with not a motor boat in sight. The M25 now crosses just downstream of Bell Weir, beside Lutyens' bridge for the by-pass, which was designed in 1937, but not built until 1959-60.

**STAINES, BOAT HOUSE REACH 1895** 35991

Sumptuous Victorian houseboats line the River Thames on 'Boat House Reach', close to the bridge. Luxurious houseboats - many of them for hire - were places for summer relaxation, allowing their inhabitants to sit on the deck and enjoy the tranquil river.

**STAINES, BOATING ON THE THAMES 1907** 57989X

Guiding a punt - and its 'fair inhabitants' - towards the graceful arches of Staines Bridge. Punting was extremely popular with both sexes from the late 1890s, especially the method of 'pricking', rather than walking the length of the punt with the punt pole.

**CHERTSEY, THE TOWN HALL 1904** 51711
The handsome lines of the Old Town Hall dominate this view of London Street. The Old Town Hall was built in 1851 by George Briand, and has an arcaded ground floor open to the street. The Crown Hotel also still stands, though the traffic has changed since this picture was taken.

**CHERTSEY**
*The Pond 1908*
This Thames-side town was once famed for its abbey, now almost entirely vanished; its stone was used for the building of Hampton Court. This idyllic view shows a once-familiar sight, horses having well-earned break from pulling their carts.

**CHERTSEY**
*Guildford Street 1908*
The action-packed scene that is a town street in Edwardian days, with plenty of people going about their business; the only traffic is horse-drawn vehicles. The butcher on the extreme right arranges his display, and the postman in the centre delivers letters.

CHERTSEY, THE POND 1908  51716

CHERTSEY, GUILDFORD STREET 1908  60929

**CHERTSEY, THE LOCK 1904** 51717
A carefully-posed study of the old lock at Chertsey, looking west, showing the lock gates partially open. This lock was replaced by the present one in 1913. The river appears devoid of traffic; this contrasts with this busy reach today, which throughout the summer buzzes with motor cruisers and holiday craft.

**CHERTSEY, THE LOCK AND THE BRIDGE 1890** 23720
This view looks east past the lock to the graceful seven-arched stone bridge. It was built around 1780 by James Paine. It had to be partially rebuilt, and was renovated in the late 1980s. The boys in the foreground have a magnificent toy sailing boat.

**CHERTSEY, THE SCHOOL 1908** 60940
Edwardian school children pose for the photographer outside their school - every one of them wearing a hat or cap. The unmetalled road has puddles from recent rain, and the pavements also appear rather muddy.

**ADDLESTONE, CROCKFORD BRIDGE 1904** 51708
A view across the River Bourne, a tributary of the Thames, with a hay cart fording the river and horse and cart and mounted horseman looking down from the bridge at the lower end of Brighton Road. Today a riverside footpath runs alongside the stream.

**ADDLESTONE, THE HOLLY TREE 1904** 51701
A beautifully-posed scene - all eyes are on the photographer - on a sunny day in the early years of the 20th century. This peaceful scene is in sharp contrast to the busy Thames valley village of today close to the M25.

**WEYBRIDGE, VIEW FROM THE LINCOLN ARMS HOTEL 1890** 23589
Once again, punting is much in evidence, with Victorian ladies sedately seated. The hamper in the right foreground points to a happy afternoon on the river. In the middle distance can be seen the confluence of the rivers Wey and Thames.

**WEYBRIDGE**
**Portmore Gateway 1903**
The open expanse of Portmore Park lay near the River Wey; it is now entirely built over - it has been thus for almost a century. It was once the setting for Ham House, given by James II to Catherine Sadley, later Countess of Dorchester and Lady Portmore. The gates survive.

◆

**WEYBRIDGE**
*Baker Street 1904*
A quiet summer scene in Weybridge at the beginning of the 20th century. On the left, the pavement is being repaired, or perhaps newly built, judging from the look of the kerbstones and lamp standard.

WEYBRIDGE, PORTMORE GATEWAY 1903   49904

WEYBRIDGE, BAKER STREET 1904   51688

**WALTON ON THAMES, THE ANGLERS 1908** 60037

Girls pose with shrimping nets outside the Swan Hotel, with its boats for hire. The coal lighters are discharging coal at the Old Town Wharf. The Swan still exists with its broad slipway, though today there are no such elegant rowing boats for hire.

**WALTON ON THAMES, THE BOATHOUSE 1899** 43040

Punting became very much a ladies' pastime, and the fame of the 'English Punt Girl' spread far and wide. In 1908 there was even an article describing her in the Travel magazine of New York. It seems that pink and white were the preferred colours to wear.

FARNHAM, THE CASTLE,1895  36127

### FARNHAM
#### *The Castle,1895*
Here we see the ruined keep of Farnham Castle, romantically clothed with vegetation. Most English monarchs from Edward I to Queen Victoria have been entertained here. Farnham Castle was the seat of the Bishop of Winchester, and now of the Bishop of Guildford. The castle was transformed by the Bishops over the years into an elegant palace.

◆

### FARNHAM
#### *Old Hop Kilns c1955*
During the 18th century hops were of prime importance to Farnham, which had five breweries and had more inns than any other town in Surrey. Now hops and breweries have gone, and there is no longer any use for the old hop kilns.

FARNHAM, OLD HOP KILNS C1955  F11027

**FARNHAM, WEST STREET 1899** 43260A

Farnham's long main street, with West Street at one end and East Street at the other and the Borough between, lies along an ancient route. West Street is renowned for its Georgian architecture - though many are older buildings re-fronted in Georgian style.

**FARNHAM, SOUTH STREET 1904** 51602a

A bustling view along South Street, which was built in 1850 and originally called New Road. It connects the town centre with the railway, and runs south from the Borough towards the River Wey. In this photograph horse-drawn carts are the only traffic.

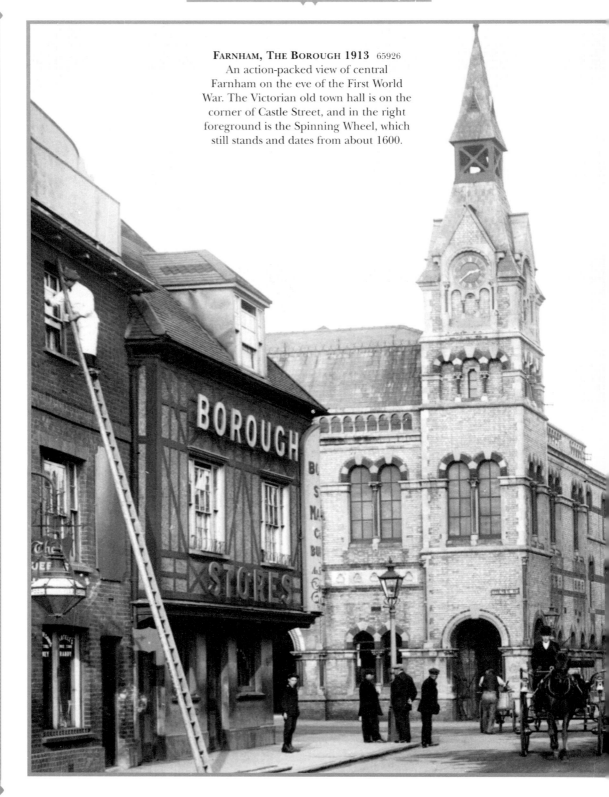

**FARNHAM, THE BOROUGH 1913** 65926
An action-packed view of central
Farnham on the eve of the First World
War. The Victorian old town hall is on the
corner of Castle Street, and in the right
foreground is the Spinning Wheel, which
still stands and dates from about 1600.

**FARNHAM, THE TOWN HALL 1935** 86762

The 1930s Town Hall replaced the Victorian building in the previous picture. This Neo-Georgian building was designed by Harold Faulkner for the landowner Mr Borelli, who aimed to return architectural harmony to the town. The Bailiff's Hall of 1674 was skilfully joined by Faulkner to his new town hall.

**FARNHAM, THE COLONNADE 1936** 87793

Here we see the colonnaded front of the Town Hall a couple of years after its completion. It was built in the Neo-Georgian style to reflect Farnham's real Georgian buildings, which were erected when the town was the largest corn market in England.

**FARNHAM, THE HOP GARDENS 1904** 51618a
In the 18th century Farnham was famous for its hop gardens, which rivalled those of Kent. Today, the hop gardens have gone, but this evocative view conjures them up again, with the tower of the parish church of St Andrew visible between the tall bines.

**FRENSHAM, THE MILITARY HOSPITAL 1917** 67977
Remodelled in neo-Tudor style in 1900 for Charrington, the London brewer, Frensham Heights was then called Frensham Hill. Memorable cricket matches were played on the cricket ground in front of the house. It served as a military hospital during the First World War, and is now a well-known school.

**FRENSHAM, BALLROOM WARD 1917** 67981
A further picture of the military hospital. The spartan nature of a hospital ward contrasts starkly with its palatial surroundings. The ballroom is rich with plaster decoration and has a particularly fine ceiling.

**FRENSHAM, THE MILITARY HOSPITAL 1917** 67984
The free-standing 'army hut' wards of the military hospital in the grounds of Frensham Heights (then known as Frensham Hill) during the First World War. Uniformed nurses stand at the open doors on this summer's day while several patients sit outside - temporarily safe from the horrors of war.

**FRENSHAM, TROOPS AT FRENSHAM 1917** F47330
A haunting and unusual picture of a marching band at Frensham during the First World War. How many of these men came back by the end of the following year? Frensham is known for its ponds and its common - now Frensham Country Park.

**CHURT, THE PRIDE OF THE VALLEY INN 1928** 80961

## CHURT
### *The Pride of the Valley Inn 1928*
In this inter-war view the camera does not quite freeze the car. The scene is one mile east of the village - the sign shows Lloyd George, who came to live in Churt in 1921 and left in 1944, the year before his death. His house, Bron y de, formerly stood nearby.

## CHURT
### *Barford Mill 1906*
The miller looks out over the pool of this old Surrey watermill at Barford, an isolated part of Churt village. Formerly there were at least three mills - one of them was a paper mill - including this corn mill, which worked until the First World War.

**CHURT, BARFORD MILL 1906** 55517

**HASLEMERE, FROM THE RECREATION GROUND 1902** 48353
Said to be the highest town in Surrey, Haslemere is 500ft up in the hills close to the borders of both Sussex and Hampshire. It was a remote spot of ironworks and farms until the coming of the railway and the arrival of the Victorian intelligentsia - including George Eliot.

**HASLEMERE, HIGH STREET 1931** 83755
The High Street is unusually wide for a Surrey village, with the Town Hall of 1814 in the centre. There is remarkably little traffic in the picture. The Dolmetsch family came to Haslemere in the 1920s, and the Dolmetsch music festival was established by Arnold Dolmetsch in 1925 to perform early music.

HASLEMERE, LORD TENNYSON'S 'ALDWORTH' 1899    43158

## HASLEMERE
### *Lord Tennyson's 'Aldworth' 1899*

Tennyson knew and loved Haslemere and the Surrey Hills. Aldworth, his former home, is in Lurgashall, Sussex, but close to Haslemere, along the now renamed Tennyson Lane. After Tennyson's death in 1892, Burne Jones designed a window in Haslemere's St Bartholomew's church as a memorial to the poet.

◆

## HASLEMERE
### *Shepherd's Hill 1888*

This steep curving road is celebrated for its row of 17th, 18th and 19th-century cottages in tile-hung brick and stucco, which stagger uphill raised above the roadway in traditional Surrey fashion. The photograph was taken in the same year that John Hutchinson opened his Haslemere Educational Museum.

HASLEMERE, SHEPHERD'S HILL 1888   H35301

**HASLEMERE, SHEPHERD'S HILL C1900**  H35401a

Another view of the pretty Shepherd's Hill cottages on their steep terrace taken some 12 years after picture No H35301, showing the curve to perfection - and a bevy of late Victorian 'missies' complete with pinafores.

**HASLEMERE, THE ALMSHOUSES, PETWORTH ROAD 1888** H35302a
Two girls pose next to the 17th-century almshouses in the Petworth Road, now the B32131. The cottages, built in 1676 from the profits of market tithes, are noted for their porches supported by wooden balustrades.

**HASLEMERE, KING'S ROAD 1909** 61435
A view looking west down King's Road from near the station towards Shottermill. Note the traction engine and trailer on the left of the picture, up Longdene Road. Today the Dolmetsch Workshop is in King's Road, and is open to visitors by appointment.

**HASLEMERE, LONGDENE 1888** H35303
A superb haymaking scene which shows the manpower once required on the land at this hill-top farm, to the south west of Haslemere. Such scenes as this have now long since vanished, not just from Surrey but from the whole of Britain.

# Index

# Frith Book Co 1999 Titles

From 2000 we aim at publishing 100 new books each year. For latest catalogue please contact Frith Book Co

| | | | |
|---|---|---|---|
| Barnstaple | 1-85937-084-5 | £12.99 | Oct 99 |
| Blackpool | 1-85937-049-7 | £12.99 | Sep 99 |
| Bognor Regis | 1-85937-055-1 | £12.99 | Sep 99 |
| Bristol | 1-85937-050-0 | £12.99 | Sep 99 |
| Cambridge | 1-85937-092-6 | £12.99 | Oct 99 |
| Cambridgeshire | 1-85937-086-1 | £14.99 | Nov 99 |
| Cheshire | 1-85937-045-4 | £14.99 | Sep 99 |
| Chester | 1-85937-090-X | £12.99 | Nov 99 |
| Chesterfield | 1-85937-071-3 | £12.99 | Sep 99 |
| Chichester | 1-85937-089-6 | £12.99 | Nov 99 |
| Cornwall | 1-85937-054-3 | £14.99 | Sep 99 |
| Cotswolds | 1-85937-099-3 | £14.99 | Nov 99 |

| | | | |
|---|---|---|---|
| Maidstone | 1-85937-056-X | £12.99 | Sep 99 |
| Northumberland & Tyne and Wear | 1-85937-072-1 | £14.99 | Sep 99 |
| North Yorkshire | 1-85937-048-9 | £14.99 | Sep 99 |
| Nottingham | 1-85937-060-8 | £12.99 | Sep 99 |
| Oxfordshire | 1-85937-076-4 | £14.99 | Oct 99 |
| Penzance | 1-85937-069-1 | £12.99 | Sep 99 |
| Reading | 1-85937-087-X | £12.99 | Nov 99 |
| St Ives | 1-85937-068-3 | £12.99 | Sep 99 |
| Salisbury | 1-85937-091-8 | £12.99 | Nov 99 |
| Scarborough | 1-85937-104-3 | £12.99 | Sep 99 |
| Scottish Castles | 1-85937-077-2 | £14.99 | Oct 99 |
| Sevenoaks and Tonbridge | 1-85937-057-8 | £12.99 | Sep 99 |
| Sheffield and S Yorkshire | 1-85937-070-5 | £12.99 | Sep 99 |
| Shropshire | 1-85937-083-7 | £14.99 | Nov 99 |
| Southampton | 1-85937-088-8 | £12.99 | Nov 99 |
| Staffordshire | 1-85937-047-0 | £14.99 | Sep 99 |
| Stratford upon Avon | 1-85937-098-5 | £12.99 | Nov 99 |
| Suffolk | 1-85937-074-8 | £14.99 | Oct 99 |
| Surrey | 1-85937-081-0 | £14.99 | Oct 99 |
| Torbay | 1-85937-063-2 | £12.99 | Sep 99 |
| Wiltshire | 1-85937-053-5 | £14.99 | Sep 99 |

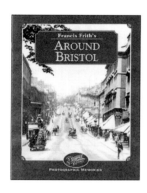

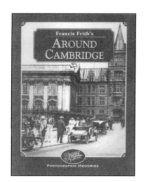

| | | | |
|---|---|---|---|
| Derby | 1-85937-046-2 | £12.99 | Sep 99 |
| Devon | 1-85937-052-7 | £14.99 | Sep 99 |
| Dorset | 1-85937-075-6 | £14.99 | Oct 99 |
| Dorset Coast | 1-85937-062-4 | £14.99 | Sep 99 |
| Dublin | 1-85937-058-6 | £12.99 | Sep 99 |
| East Anglia | 1-85937-059-4 | £14.99 | Sep 99 |
| Eastbourne | 1-85937-061-6 | £12.99 | Sep 99 |
| English Castles | 1-85937-078-0 | £14.99 | Oct 99 |
| Essex | 1-85937-082-9 | £14.99 | Nov 99 |
| Falmouth | 1-85937-066-7 | £12.99 | Sep 99 |
| Hampshire | 1-85937-064-0 | £14.99 | Sep 99 |
| Hertfordshire | 1-85937-079-9 | £14.99 | Nov 99 |
| Isle of Man | 1-85937-065-9 | £14.99 | Sep 99 |
| Liverpool | 1-85937-051-9 | £12.99 | Sep 99 |

**British Life A Century Ago**

246 x 189mm 144pp, hardback. Black and white Lavishly illustrated with photos from the turn of the century, and with extensive commentary. It offers a unique insight into the social history and heritage of bygone Britain.

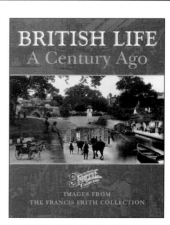

1-85937-103-5 £17.99

# Available from your local bookshop or from the publisher

# FRITH PRODUCTS & SERVICES

Francis Frith would doubtless be pleased to know that the pioneering publishing venture he started in 1860 still continues today. More than a hundred and thirty years later, The Francis Frith Collection continues in the same innovative tradition and is now one of the foremost publishers of vintage photographs in the world. Some of the current activities include:

### Interior Decoration

Today Frith's photographs can be seen framed and as giant wall murals in thousands of pubs, restaurants, hotels, banks, retail stores and other public buildings throughout the country. In every case they enhance the unique local atmosphere of the places they depict and provide reminders of gentler days in an increasingly busy and frenetic world.

### Product Promotions

Frith products have been used by many major companies to promote the sales of their own products or to reinforce their own history and heritage. Brands include Hovis bread, Courage beers, Scots Porage Oats, Colman's mustard, Cadbury's foods, Mellow Birds coffee, Dunhill pipe tobacco, Guinness, and Bulmer's Cider.

### Genealogy and Family History

As the interest in family history and roots grows world-wide, more and more people are turning to Frith's photographs of Great Britain for images of the towns, villages and streets where their ancestors lived; and, of course, photographs of the churches and chapels where their ancestors were christened, married and buried are an essential part of every genealogy tree and family album.

A series of easy-to-use CD Roms is planned for publication, and an increasing number of Frith photographs will be able to be viewed on specialist genealogy sites. A growing range of Frith books will be available on CD.

### The Internet

Already thousands of Frith photographs can be viewed and purchased on the internet. By the end of the year 2000 some 60,000 Frith photographs will be available on the internet. The number of sites is constantly expanding, each focussing on different products and services from the Collection.

Some of the sites are listed below.

www.townpages.co.uk
www.familystorehouse.com
www.britannia.com
www.icollector.com
www.barclaysquare.co.uk
www.cornwall-online.co.uk

For background information on the Collection look at the two following sites:

www.francisfrith.com
www.francisfrith.co.uk

### Frith Products

All Frith photographs are available Framed or just as Mounted Prints, and can be ordered from the address below. From time to time other products - Address Books, Calendars, Table Mats, Postcards etc - are available.

### The Frith Collectors' Guild

In response to the many customers who enjoy collecting Frith photographs we have created the Frith Collectors' Guild. Members are entitled to a range of benefits, including a regular magazine, special discounts and special limited edition products.

**For further information:** if you would like further information on any of the above aspects of the Frith business please contact us at the address below:

**The Francis Frith Collection, Frith's Barn, Teffont, Salisbury, Wiltshire England SP3 5QP.**
Tel: +44 (0) 1722 716 376  Fax: +44 (0) 1722 716 881   Email: frithbook.co.uk

# To receive your FREE Mounted Print

*Cut out this Voucher and return it with your remittance for £1.50 to cover postage and handling. Choose any photograph included in this book. Your SEPIA print will be A4 in size, and mounted in a cream mount with burgundy rule lines, overall size 14 x 11 inches.*

## Order additional Mounted Prints at HALF PRICE (only £7.49 each*)

If there are further pictures you would like to order, possibly as gifts for friends and family, acquire them at half price (no additional postage and handling required).

## Have your Mounted Prints framed*

For an additional £14.95 per print you can have your chosen Mounted Print framed in an elegant polished wood and gilt moulding, overall size 16 x 13 inches (no additional postage and handling required).

---

**\* IMPORTANT!**
**These special prices are only available if ordered using the original voucher on this page (no copies permitted) and at the same time as your free Mounted Print, for delivery to the same address**

---

## Voucher for FREE and Reduced Price Frith Prints

| Picture no. | Page number | Qty | Mounted @ £7.49 | Framed + £14.95 | Total Cost |
|---|---|---|---|---|---|
| | | 1 | **Free of charge*** | £ | £ |
| | | | £ | £ | £ |
| | | | £ | £ | £ |
| | | | £ | £ | £ |
| | | | £ | £ | £ |
| | | | £ | £ | £ |

**Title: SURREY**
081-0

| | |
|---|---|
| * Post & handling | £1.50 |
| **Total Order Cost** | £ |

*Please do not photocopy this voucher. Only the original is valid, so please cut it out and return it to us.*

I enclose a cheque / postal order for £ . . . . . . . . . .
made payable to 'The Francis Frith Collection'
OR please debit my Mastercard / Visa / Switch / Amex card

Number . . . . . . . . . . . . . . . . . . . . . . . . . . . . .

Expires . . . . . . . . . .  Signature . . . . . . . . . . . . . . . . . . . . . .

Name  Mr/Mrs/Ms . . . . . . . . . . . . . . . . . . . . . . . . . . . . . . . . . .

Address . . . . . . . . . . . . . . . . . . . . . . . . . . . . . . . . . . . . . . . . .

. . . . . . . . . . . . . . . . . . . . . . . . . . . . . . . . . . . . . . . . . . . . . . .

. . . . . . . . . . . . . . . . . . . . . . . . . . . . . . . . . . . . . . . . . . . . . . .

. . . . . . . . . . . . . . . . . . . . . . . . . . . Postcode . . . . . . . . . . . . . . .

Daytime Tel No . . . . . . . . . . . . . . . . . . . . . . . . .   Valid to 31/12/01

---

# Frith Collectors' Guild

*From time to time we publish a magazine of news and stories about Frith photographs and further special offers of Frith products. If you would like 12 months FREE membership, please return this form and we will send you a New Member Pack.*

*Send completed forms to:*
**The Francis Frith Collection, Frith's Barn, Teffont, Salisbury, Wiltshire SP3 5QP**

# The Francis Frith Collectors' Guild

I would like to receive the New Members Pack offering 12 months FREE membership.
081-0

Name  Mr/Mrs/Ms . . . . . . . . . . . . . . . . . . . . . . . . . . . . . . . . . .

Address . . . . . . . . . . . . . . . . . . . . . . . . . . . . . . . . . . . . . . . . .

. . . . . . . . . . . . . . . . . . . . . . . . . . . . . . . . . . . . . . . . . . . . . . .

. . . . . . . . . . . . . . . . . . . . . Postcode . . . . . . . . . . . . . . . . . . .